I0471743

The Time that People *FORGOT*

...the 10 Laws of achieving more – and still having weekends off...

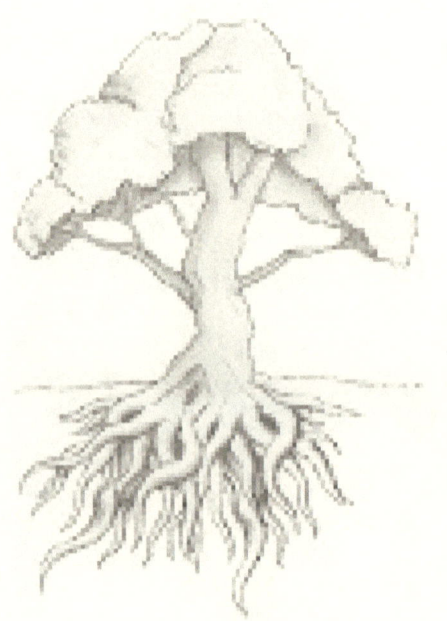

David Holland MBA

© Copyright 2012 David Holland

978-1-291-22553-2

All rights reserved

Contents

INTRODUCTION 5

THE 10 LAWS 10

The Law of Management 10

The Law of Vision 15

The Law of Efficiency and Productivity 27

The Law of Circadian Rhythms 32

The Law of Knowledge 41

The Law of Peak Condition 48

The Law of Planning 53

The Law of Urgent, Important and Facebook 64

The Law of Discipline 69

The Law of NO 76

ABOUT RESULTS RULES OK 80

The Time that People FORGOT

...the 10 Laws of achieving more - and still having weekends off...

Introduction

This book is dedicated to the Team at the Bank of New York Mellon in Luxembourg – the reason it was written at all is because of a question I was asked during a recent training session there.

I was asked;

"Do we have anything to help with Time Management..?"

Of the 38 Books we have published so far, there was nothing specifically to do with Time Management - I never seemed to have time to write one – *but as you can see, there is now*.

This book was started on the 1st November 2012 and will be presented to the Team at BNY Mellon, Luxembourg next time we deliver an event, which is scheduled for 13th November.

So this is an exercise in speed writing – I really couldn't imagine trying to explain to the Team that I didn't complete the book on Time Management because I didn't have time.

So for anyone interested in being more productive, getting more done and having weekends off – please read on. To the Team at BNY Mellon – thank you for the challenge, I hope you enjoy the book…

We are all given the gift of Time on Earth – some of us only get a few precious hours before we are invited to leave, others are fortunate to extend our welcome to decades. According to the CIA World Fact Book 2011 – if you live in Monaco your life expectancy at birth will be 89.73 years, whereas in if you live in Swaziland your life expectancy at birth is just 31.88 years.

So clearly the first thing you should do in order to manage your time better and have the opportunity of getting more done, is to move to Monaco. Macau and San Marino are pretty good too, ranking 2nd and 3rd in the list respectively – in fact anywhere that begins with M or has a F1 Grand Prix looks to be a safe bet.

If you are living in Swaziland – probably best if you just read this introduction and finish the rest of the book when you are safely in Monaco – otherwise you may simply run out of time…

So let's assume that we have about 80 years to live, this means we have 700,000 hours to invest in our lives – we spend around 1/3 of the time asleep 1/3 working and the rest is used to get to and from work, worry about work or take in the visual anaesthetic we call Television; and of course to live our lives.

How we invest this time is the key to our happiness, contribution and legacy to the world; remember each day is a present, and the future is promised to no one. The Chinese have a saying that the perfect time to plant a tree is 30 years ago, and today – whatever you choose to do in life, make sure you do it today.

Starting out as an Apprentice at the Royal Small Arms Factory in Enfield, London, I was fortunate to be able to learn the skills required for the Design, Production and Testing of Assault Rifles, Sniper Rifles and Cannon up to 30mm bore…

I also had the opportunity of working alongside and learning from some of the best Engineers and Tradesmen in the world. Learning my craft in an establishment that was at the time part of the Ministry of Defence, also meant that I came to understand the importance of discipline.

Once at lunchtime I was walking across the "square" to go to the canteen for lunch – I had decided to leave my department 2 minutes early, to beat the queues – and I was spotted by the dreaded Apprentice Manager.

Leaving early was clearly not OK…!!

I was put on report and given a "punishment block" to complete. This punishment block took me 7 days to complete and involved, finishing using hand tools only, the production of a block of metal that was "exactly" 2 Inches long and 2 Inch diameter. And it was to be made out of steel that is used for Gun Barrels – so tough as well, with a surface finish that was to be hand lapped to Ra 16 – very smooth...!!

Now, all the engineers out there will know that there is no such thing as "exact" when it comes to measurements – so I had a "tolerance of +/- 0.001 Inch to work to. Human hair is around 0.004 Inches thick, and this tolerance applied to not just the length, but the roundness too...

After 7 days of working on this – it was finally accepted and I was allowed to return to normal duties.

The lesson I learned as a 17 year old was that timing matters – if I agree to be somewhere at a certain time, then I need to be there; not 1 minute of 5 minutes late but on time every time. This has stayed with me ever since – and being "irritatingly punctual" has been a trademark of mine ever since. If I agree to be somewhere at a certain time I will be there, probably 10 minutes early too..

So why this story...?

Because what I have come to realise is that there is a global phenomenon called "local time". Wherever in the world I am fortunate enough to go there is always a "local time" syndrome meaning people arrive late for meetings, calls, appointments, seminars, workshops and conferences.

In France it is called French Time, in Luxembourg it is called Luxembourg Time and in Mexico it called Mexican Time in fact choose any country in the world and you can have Xxxx Time – in other words, there is a global excuse for being late.

So as a Prologue to this book – BE ON TIME for everything – doing this alone will transform your results and develop your personal brand as the person who can be trusted and relied upon.

The 10 Laws.

To achieve more in the time that we have – we cannot simply treat the symptoms of the disease; the apparent lack of time. We have to confront the contributory factors that result in there apparently not being enough time.

So rather than simply recommend a time plan, and default diary – both of which will appear in this book – we will be going much deeper into the psychology of achievement, personal supporting strategies that when applied consistently will result in you achieving more than you imagined with less than you believed you had.

The Law of Management.

First, the bad news…

Time cannot be managed – you can only manage yourself within the time you have.

"Time is a dimension in which events can be ordered from the past through the present into the future, and also the measure of durations of events and the intervals between them…"

Source; Wikipedia.

Time flows at a constant rate, we measure the flow of time by allocating packets of it, named such as seconds, minutes, hours, days and years. In fact, time is one of the few constants we have in our lives; it is the same for everyone, it doesn't vary in quality and its pace never changes.

This is why it can't be managed – according to the Oxford Dictionary at www.oxforddictionaries.com the definition of Management is;

"The process of dealing with or controlling things or people…"

Time is not a "thing", processes are things, money is a thing – we can have direct influence over them and therefore we can manage them.

Here lies the frustration for most of us. We like to be in control, to be able to influence our environment, and manage our lives. Time, however, doesn't play this game with us – it defies our attempts at control by insisting that the sands flow at a constant rate through the hourglass – even conspiring to give the impression that fun times go quickly and hard times last longer.

We have to let go of the hope for control here – we have no influence over the amount of time we are given, or the speed at which it flows away from us – what we do have control over is ourselves.

As a Coach I am always interested in the best excuses people use for not achieving what they set out to do. In fact, with some Clients, I give them a comprehensive list of the best excuses I have heard for not getting things done – and tell them that these are not allowed to be used in our work together.

Here are a few of the most popular excuses – and solutions;

A. **I don't have time** – yes you do. You simply choose to allocate it to something else that is easier, requires less effort and probably involves Alcohol, Food or Television; possibly all three.

B. **I can't afford it** – yes you can. You have chosen to sacrifice the application, dedication and discipline required to make more money and chosen to wallow in self-pity and delusional, self-gratifying negativity.

C. **I'm not ready yet** – yes you are. Instead of achieving your life's dream, you have decided to wait until the conditions are perfect. The conditions are only perfect for one second – and that second is NOW. Procrastination is the single biggest killer of achievement.

D. **I'm scared** – we are all scared, get over it. The world is a scary place, for a start it is full of humans, the scariest species known to man. Fear is simply your subconscious giving you an excuse to be lazy. If you weren't scared what would you do – if you couldn't fail what would you attempt..?

E. **I can't** – applies to a multitude of entry level excuses, usually followed by a mediocre justification for mediocrity starting with the word because. If you had to be amazing you would be – if the incentive to achieve is strong enough you will find a way.

Goal Oriented
Responsible
Energetic
Enthusiastic
Nurturing

Reasons
Evidence
Doubtful

There are loads more and you can probably add some of your favourites to the list, but you get the picture – the Law of Management states that we have to Manage Ourselves first.

Management of Self takes discipline and courage – it involves taking away our favourite excuses and replacing them with experiences and actions. It also means that the one excuse that has served us so well – *lack of time* – has to be removed from our vocabulary.

There is no such thing as lack of time; only the requirement for the rearrangement of resources within it.

As a guide, consider the model in the image. I see people who live their lives in the RED zone.

They have plenty of Reasons why they are not able to achieve their goals (if they have any...) or why their lives are so tough and disappointing.

They back up their Reasons with Evidence that justifies and supports their contention that they should stay where they are.

And finally they are Doubtful – about themselves, their environment, their potential and ability to make positive change. It is the oppression from within that is more powerful than any perceived Orwellian conspiracy theory – what we tell ourselves about ourselves is true.

Management of Self requires us to operate in the GREEN zone – more details are covered in the following 9 Laws – but you can see the difference. Operating here requires discipline and removal of the Reasons and Excuses – it really depends if you prefer the pain of discipline or the pain of regret.

Top Tips from this Chapter...

- **You can't manage Time** – only yourself and what you choose to do with it.
- **Excuses don't count** – take responsibility for your activity and output.
- **Lack of Time** – doesn't exist, remove it from your vocabulary.
- **Lack of Time** – no such thing, only lack of Management.

Notes and Action Points

The Law of Vision

When we lived in the USA – I promised myself that I would own a big ridiculous V8 SUV and Harley Davidson. The V8 objective was achieved through the acquisition of a Ford Expedition 5.4l Eddie Bauer, and the Harley objective was achieved when I took delivery of my Night Rod Special – the water-cooled one with the engine designed by Porsche.

I bought the bike without ever having sat on a motorcycle before – not even a scooter. We hired a trailer and took it in to the desert north of Las Vegas, on the outskirts of the huge Nellis US Air Force Base. I looked up how the controls worked and figured that it must be relatively straight forwards to ride and control the machine. I had always wondered what it would be like to buy a powerful bike and just get on it without any training or supervision, and then see what happens.

This was in effect a dream come true – here was I riding the most powerful production bike that Harley Davidson make, up and down a deserted road in the Nevada sunshine.

All was fine – it took the bike up to 70 or 80mph and spent the day blasting up and down the track – objective completed.

Now, in order to take the bike on public roads of course I needed a licence. So I booked a course at Las Vegas Harley Davidson and attended a four day intensive program that would make me safe and legal.

If you go to Las Vegas, the Harley Davidson dealers at either Red Rock on South Rainbow and West Sahara or Las Vegas on East Sahara and South Eastern are definitely worth a visit – even if you don't like bikes – go for the people and the atmosphere…

As part of the training we were to ride 500cc Buell bikes to learn manoeuvring and road safety principles – so we were taken to an empty car park at the side of the Harley Dealer. In this car park – there was a single light stand in the middle that supported the flood lights for night time illumination. It was embedded in a large concrete block which was painted with yellow and black stripes.

Assembled in the car park, our instructor gave us the first rule of riding a motorbike.

"Where you look is where you will go, or what you look at is what you will hit…"

If you focus on a clear exit to a bend then that is where you will go – your physiology will instruct the bike to take you that way. Equally if you focus on an obstacle such as a tree – that is what you will hit, your physiology will guide you there too.

He told us that there were therefore two things in that car park that we should not look at; the concrete light stand, and him…

In essence, what he was saying was that whatever you focus on or give your attention to will become manifest to you; the same rules apply in life as they do to riding a motorbike.

> At a recent Conference in the UK, I was explaining the power of focus - what you focus on will become manifest to you.
>
> When Lynn was pregnant, I asked the audience what they thought I started to see lots of, for example…
>
> The answer "Hookers..?"
>
> I clearly need to ask better questions …

Two riders managed to hit the concrete block during the training – this is a one acre car park with a 3m cube striped concrete block in the middle. Some people find the obstacles while some find the pathway – depends on where your vision is applied.

If you choose to focus on opportunity, achievement and positive outcomes then you will find that they start to show up – your physiology will guide you towards them. If you focus on the obstacles (excuses, or reasons…) then you will hit them too.

It's all a matter of perspective – I could have used the fact that I had no licence or experience on a bike as a great excuse for not getting one for example. My focus was the bike and I didn't see the obstacles – when they became clear, they were simple to overcome.

So in order to achieve more – have a Vision…

How does this help with getting more done within the time that you have…?

It prevents the distractions – someone working "on purpose" is un-stoppable – they have passion, energy and enthusiasm. In fact they display all the GREEN traits on the image describes in the 1st chapter.

It's as if the most productive day of the year – usually the day before you go on holiday – shows up every day. When there is a deadline, goal or objective that is compelling to you then you will be amazed at what you can get done in the time that you have.

The Vision should be personal to you. If you own your own business then your professional and personal goals are so intertwined that they cannot be separated – they define who you are and more importantly why you do what you do.

If you work within a company, the same rules apply –just recognise that your personal goals need to be in alignment or at least fully supported by your professional goals.

Having clarity of purpose will enable you to achieve more, it removes procrastination, encourages you to inspire those around you and invigorate your work such that the pace of your work flow increases.

Types of Vision…

When you go into a restaurant, you will usually be given the menu and a few minutes to choose what you want. When you are asked what you want, here is what you tend NOT to say…

"Well, I don't want the pork and I definitely don't want the veal, the chicken looks bland and the last time I had fish I was ill…"

What usually happens, and it does depend who you go to dinner with, is something like this…

"I'll have the filet steak please…"

"Certainly, how would you like your Filet Steak cooked..?"

"Oh – rare please…"

"What potatoes would you like; dauphinoise, au gratin or fries..?"

"Dauphinoise please..."

"And what sauce would you like; pepper, café de Paris, or béarnaise..?"

"Café de Paris please…"

What happens is that rather than saying what you don't want you ask for what you do want. In fact you are encouraged to be really specific – not just a steak, but the preparation and the trimmings too.

This is a towards type goal as opposed to an away from goal which is simply clarity about what to avoid – not what to aim for…

Plenty of people have away from goals – they know exactly what they don't want. They want to get away from credit cards, debts, poor relationships etc. What they tend to have less clarity around is what they actually do want.

The challenge with an away from goal is that it is short term. Let's look at a common reason people start their own business for example.

A common reason is that they want to get away from employment; they want to get away from the politics and bureaucracy that was imposed on them within their company.

This objective is achieved the instant that they resign and start their own company. But then without a future objective in mind they will simply drift along – the objective has been met, the away from goal has been achieved. This is why so many new businesses don't make it – not because they are not fundamentally good businesses, but because they have achieved the only objective that the owner had; to get away from employment.

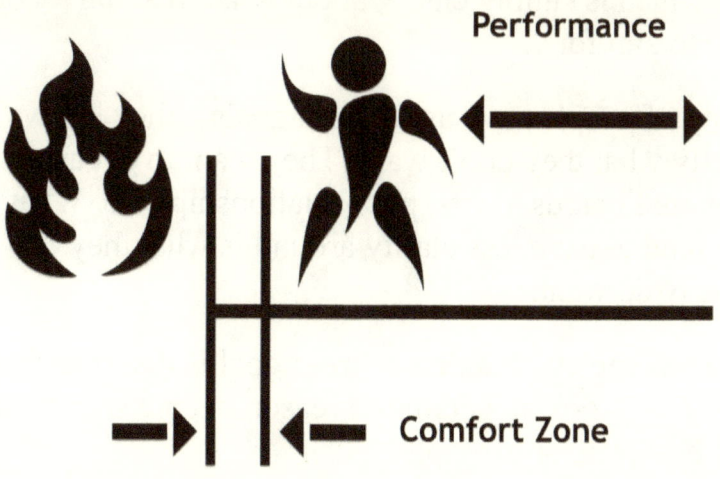

In the picture, imagine that the fire represents what it is that you want to get away from. This could be a relationship, job, debt or any uncomfortable situation.

If the situation gets really bad then you will react and step away from the heat; take action – but only until the heat becomes bearable or comfortable.

Then you relax and stability returns. An away from goal only motivates us when the tough situations get worse – there is a danger that we go through life tolerating mediocrity until we are "forced" by circumstance to change and do something different.

When the heat is reduced – we simply go back to a different level of mediocrity that feels comfortable to us. We never actually get close to achieving our peak performance because we never need to...

When however we have a compelling towards type goal, one that both excites and inspires us and those around us, we have the opportunity of raising our game and our standards of performance accordingly – to achieve something amazing we have to do something extraordinary.

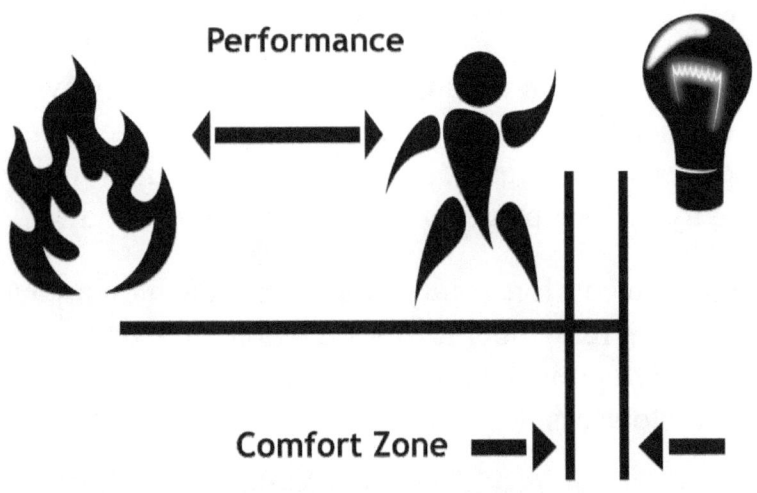

The heat is still in the picture, but is not the heat that moves us anymore it is the attraction to the light on the right of the image that compels us to achieve.

There is still a comfort zone associated with the achievement of these types of objectives, and one that is as dangerous as the one that appears at the other end of the scale.

In Wagner's 1859 Opera Tristan and Isolde, arguably influenced by Schopenhauer there is a scene where although Tristan has accomplished so much he is not happy or content. When asked why this is, Isolde responds – "because he has lost the one thing that kept him alive – his dream..."

Now, while Schopenhauer may argue that the only way for us to achieve inner peace is for us to renounce our desires – my belief and experience is that it is the achievement of our desires that prevents us having the inner peace to which he refers, and anyway being peaceful is not on my agenda yet...

What I mean here is simply that the chase is always better than the catch – it is the journey that excites us – indeed when we get close to our goals we may find we actually self-sabotage so we never reach the end...

We have a comfort zone just in front of achieving our objective – remember it is not the objective that motivates us it is the possibility of achieving it, and the journey towards it.

There is a myth that we need to set "Big Fat Hairy Audacious Goals" – no we don't. We need to set a series of Inspiring Goals – with each new Goal being prescribed just before the achievement of the current one. I don't believe that anything big fat and hairy is particularly attractive anyway. ☺

The challenge (not allowed to say problem apparently...) with setting huge goals is not the goal itself but the vantage point from which the goal is chosen.

There is a Jewish saying "to a worm inside horseradish, the world is horseradish". Or put more simply perhaps – we only know what we can see.

When setting Goals we will choose them on the basis of our current understanding and beliefs – we may therefore not choose the optimal goal. The best goals become apparent as the journey unfolds – that is why a series of goals will be much more relevant than a single fat hairy one selected when one is contained within the metaphorical horseradish.

So in summary – your achievements will be the consequence of the quality of your goals. When you have a non-negotiable goal you will be more engaged, and motivated to make things happen – you will be working on purpose, every day will be the day before the holidays.

Top Tips from this Chapter...

- **Vision** – what you focus on will become manifest to you.
- **To Want or Not to Want** – focus on what you DO want not what you DON'T.
- **Goals Change** – think bigger the farther you go.
- **Comfort Zones** – will kill your development.

Notes and Action Points

The Law of Efficiency and Productivity

I trained as a Production Engineer, involved in the batch manufacturing of assault rifles, machine guns and cannon. My job was relatively straight forwards; I had to balance three aspects of the production process.

a. **Quality** – maintaining the quality of the components produced such that the assembled weapons were fit for purpose. Quality was measured by gauges and specialist measuring devices to ensure that the manufacturing tolerances, finishes and properties were achieved to an acceptable level; the amount of scrap or rework was kept within target ranges.

b. **Efficiency** – the attendance and application of the machines and people under my control. Efficiency is a measure of the application of resources compared with their total availability.

For example;

Imagine a worker is employed for 8 hours per day, 5 days per week. Over a 52 week year the worker is available for work for 52 x 40hrs = 2080 hrs.

This is the maximum that a person can work without overtime. However, it is unlikely that the worker will be engaged in work continuously for each of the 2080 hours – here's what can change the value.

I.   Holidays – assume 28 Days @ 8 hrs. per day = 224 hrs.

II.   Sickness – assume 10 Days @ 8Hrs. per day = 80 hrs.

III. Waiting time – assumed annual value = 200 hrs.

IV.   Wandering about – assumed annual value = 200 hrs.

V.   Rest Breaks – assumed annual value = 150 hrs.

VI.   Chatting – assumed annual value = 200 hrs.

VII. Procrastination – assumed annual value = 200 hrs.

VIII. Mistakes / Rework – assumed annual value = 200 hrs.

Now these figures are made up – but in reality, they are not that far away from actual results in some organisations.

So given the data above, we can work out the actual number of hours that can be applied to productive work as a percentage of the total available – a measure of productivity.

Efficiency % = (Productive Hrs. / Available Hrs.) / 100
Efficiency % = (576 Hrs. / 2080 Hrs.) /100
Efficiency = 28%

So based on the data – this business or department on average is just 28% efficient – in other words, 72% of the available time is being allocated to activities other than productive work.

c. **Productivity** – the rate of output achieved for every unit of resource utilised.

For example, one of my production lines was involved with the manufacture of firing pins for assault rifles – and I would measure the productivity on the basis of output per hour.

If during a year, using the data above a team of 10 staff produced 250,000 firing pins – this is how we would calculate the Productivity of the line.

Productivity = Total Parts Produced / Productive Hours Utilised.

Productivity = 250,000 / (576 hrs. x 10 workers)

Productivity = 250,000 / 5760 hrs.

Productivity = 43 components per hour

This equates to a total of 1.38 minutes to produce each firing pin.

My challenge as a Production Engineer was to improve these results and therefore produce the Firing Pins to the required quality standards whilst improving both productivity and efficiency.

Now, if I asked the workers if they could achieve more – they would probably say that they didn't have time to make any more pins – they were busy already.

When we look at "time management" – which we now know is impossible, we tend to focus on how busy we are, not on how Productive or Efficient we actually are.

There is a clear relationship between the three aspects of Production – there is a fourth aspect that involves the degree of risk and danger to employees too – for now I am assuming that all Health and Safety regulations are being fully complied with. Again this may or may not be the case in some organisations.

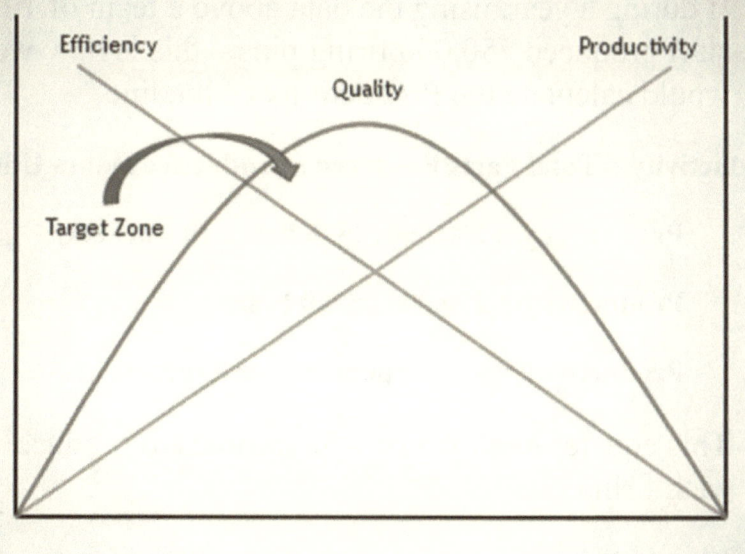

The chart shows the relationship between the levels of Efficiency, Productivity and Quality expressed as a graph. Without going in to all the intricate details there are a couple of Rules of Production that are worth bearing in mind.

I. As Efficiency Increases – Productivity may Decline after a certain point indicated by where the lines cross – workers may not work faster just because they are productive for more time, in fact they may tend to slow down if they feel that "chatting" and "wandering around" time has been taken away from them.

II. As Productivity Increases – Quality may Decline when the curve begins to fall – speed is the enemy of Quality, so as the focus shifts to increase output, so must the emphasis be increased on the process and systems involved such that quality is maintained at acceptable levels.

III. As Quality Increases – Productivity may Decline – the converse of pt. 2 above.

So the question we have to ask ourselves when it comes to achieving more, is not simply look to do more – but look at how our time is actually being invested.

What your actual Efficiency – how much time is really spent in the "wandering around" category – how much of your teams time is spent here...?

What is your productivity – are you working at optimum levels, or is quality suffering and causing rework and delays.

These two areas alone will free up time to be invested in productive activities – and they are so simple to measure and improve. This is a great place to start.

Top Tips from this Chapter...

- **Efficiency** – are you actually applying yourself 100%.
- **Productivity** – are your working Smart or just Hard.
- **Quality** – being just right is OK.
- **Sacrifice** – what needs to be sacrificed in order to achieve more..?

<u>Notes and Action Points</u>

The Law of Circadian Rhythms.

The Law of What…?

This is the study of what we call the Body Clock – a biological process with an oscillation period of about 24 hrs. The rhythm is what is called endogenous, meaning that the rhythm repeats without the need for external influences.

The word is derived from the Latin Circa meaning about and Diem meaning Day – About a Day…

These rhythms indicate when we should normally be sleeping, become most alert, are most coordinated etc. These patterns define our behaviour and ability to perform at the highest levels of productivity and efficiency.

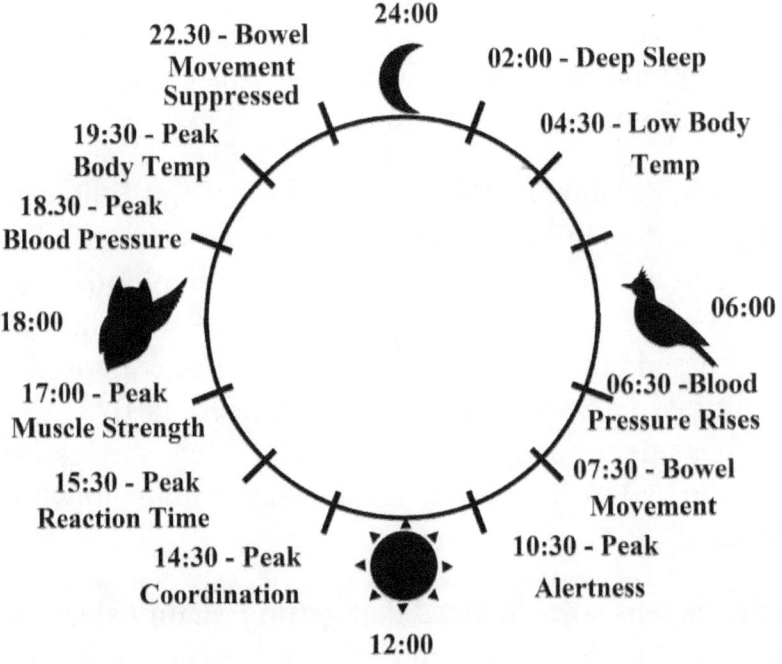

Working and living in harmony with your Circadian Rhythm will allow you to be more effective in the time that you have. Duration and Quality of sleep is critical to our ability to function at our peak.

Step 1 – recognise your personal pattern. Whilst the Rhythm is consistent, it may be that yours is "adjusted". Are you a Lark or an Owl for example – do you operate at your best in the Mornings or the Evenings..?

I am more creative and productive in the Mornings; however, I am better on stage in the afternoon and evenings for example. I also recognise that if I don't get 8 hours sleep – my mood, attitude and ability to create, coach or present declines dramatically.

To check your own Rhythm simply keep a note of your activities and levels of energy at different times of the day – and check on the amount of sleep you are actually getting. Keep a record and over time you will discover your optimal pattern, once you have this pattern – do whatever you can to stick to it.

In 2008, Arianna Huffington – President and Editor in Chief of the Huffington Post – woke up in her office, lying on the floor with her face covered in blood. She had become so exhausted through lack of sleep that she had passed out and banged her head as she collapsed resulting in a broken cheekbone and needing five stitches under her eyebrow. It was then that she realised that she had to "renew her estranged relationship with sleep…"

Arianna was so convinced that getting quality sleep is beneficial to not only productivity and efficiency, but quality and enjoyment of life that she had beds installed in the offices of the Huffington Post so that her team could take a nap when they needed to. More information about Arianna and her "Sleep your Way to the Top" campaign, can be found online at http://en.wikipedia.org/wiki/Arianna_Huffington

In the UK, the Great British Sleep Survey was undertaken between March 2010 and June 2012, with a total of 20,184 people taking part.

The results and findings of the study show that poor sleepers are;

- Three times more likely to struggle to concentrate.

- Twice as likely to suffer from fatigue.

- Twice as likely to struggle to be productive.

In 1998 as part of my MBA program I published my dissertation creatively titled "Managing Shift Work" – unsurprisingly you have probably never heard of this document, even though it is a work of genius – it got me a pass grade anyway…

What is Sleep…?

During periods of being awake, the body will burn oxygen and food, thus providing the energy for the range of physical and mental activities. This "catabolic" state, in which more energy is spent than conserved, uses up the body resources; during this period the action of the stimulatory hormones, principally Adrenaline (epinephrine) and natural Corticosteroids are dominant.

During sleep, the body moves into an "anabolic" state during which, energy conservation, repair and growth processes take over. The levels of Adrenaline and Corticosteroids reduce and the body will produce growth hormone.

When the ability to measure electrical activity in the brain was used to record humans sleep, researchers found that sleep was not just a shutting off of the brain. Instead they found a variety of brain wave patterns that repeat themselves during the night. These patterns form what is often called "sleep architecture".

Normal sleep has a very specific architecture. Sleep can be divided in to five identifiable stages.

When people are relaxed in bed with their eyes closed, the brain produces a pattern known as Alpha Waves. When they fall asleep, the brain waves change to reduced voltage, lower frequency pattern, which indicates that they have entered Stage 1 Sleep.

After 5 minutes in Stage 1 Sleep, two new types of brain waves emerge. The presence of distinct waves called K Complexes with bursts of high frequency activity indicates that Stage 2 Sleep has been reached. As the sleep period continues for another 30 to 40 minutes, the brain waves slowdown in frequency, but increase in amplitude. When they slow down to around two cycles per second, the person will have entered Stage 3 Sleep. This is also called Delta Sleep, because the slow waves are known as Delta Waves.

As the brain begins to produce mostly Delta Waves the person is considered to be in Stage 4 Sleep.

After about 80 to 90 minutes of sleep, the Delta Waves begin to subside and return to a brain pattern similar to being awake, even though people will be in the deepest stage of sleep. The paradox is called REM (rapid eye movement) sleep. The brain is alive and lucid and the person will experience their first vivid dream, and enter the first REM stage. As the night progresses, the cycle is repeated 4 or 5 times.

In order for a person to feel fully rested and alert, this architecture must not be disrupted. However, there are a number of factors that can disturb the pattern. Changing ones sleep time from day to night and back again, as rotating shift workers must do is one of them.

In order that any individual feels well rested and alert, the five stages have to occur in their proper proportions and sequence, sleep specialists who treat people with sleep disorders have identified that underlying virtually every complaint is disruption to the natural pattern of sleep.

In a technical sense, all shift workers have a sleep disorder. In 1979 the Association of Sleep Disorders published the first comprehensive classification of sleep and arousal disorders. Under the section "Disorders of Sleep – Wake Schedule" they include the diagnostic "Persistent Frequently Changing Sleep – Wake Schedule" this syndrome can be the consequence of several contributory factors, one of which would be rotating shift work. Another of which would be short sleep periods, or periods of low quality sleep induced by stress, alcohol, stimulants or disruption.

Step 2 – get quality sleep. Being prepared for work is probably the best way to achieve more and manage oneself within the time available. I know that I need a minimum of 7 hours sleep to be at my best. The sleep needs to be between 11.00 and 06.00 ideally – this allows me to match my sleep pattern and quality with my Circadian Rhythm.

Recently, I was invited to speak at a conference in Nigeria. The event was on a Friday and I would need to be on stage from 09.30 for around 2 hours, presenting to an audience of local entrepreneurs and business leaders. The challenge was that I was onstage in Luxembourg until 17.00 on the Thursday – how could I possibly be in Lagos on stage the next morning.

True to my nature, I accepted the booking and then sought to "make it happen"…

Flying to London Heathrow from Luxembourg on the Thursday evening, I would catch the overnight flight with Arik Air to Lagos, sleep on the plane and be refreshed and ready for the event on the Friday morning.

Seemed like a good idea at the time – however, the flight was noisy and I got around 3 hours sleep, all of poor quality. I arrived in Lagos at around 06.00, went to the hotel, got freshened up and was on stage for 09.00. I made it…

I know when a presentation goes well; I recognise the connection with the audience, the energy and the participation. This presentation went OK – I was on caffeine and adrenaline. The lack of sleep affected my performance, and whilst I got away with it – the next day I was truly miserable.

Step 3 – avoid the chemicals. Sleeping pills, depressants such as alcohol or stimulants such as caffeine will disrupt your quality of sleep. This is why even if you have had eight hours sleep after a bottle of Chianti – you will feel awful; not just because of the alcohols effect on your body, but the effect it has on your ability to have quality sleep.

Top Tips from this Chapter...

- **Sleep** – you need the right amount at the right time.
- **Drink** – affects sleep quality and architecture.
- **Stimulants** – will affect the quality of your sleep.
- **Rhythm** – is your life in sympathy with your Rhythm..?

<u>Notes and Action Points</u>

The Law of Knowledge.

As a young Engineer, my work involved the manufacture of Assault Rifles and weapons for the British Military. For those that have read my first book **Life Rules OK**, you will know about the time I met "David Watts" on the train to Liverpool Street – and how I decided to volunteer for opportunities that became available.

One of these opportunities was to modify a particular weapon system in readiness for the upcoming Falklands War back in 1982. Our forces were due to deploy and we needed to modify some equipment such that it suited the anticipated environment they would encounter in theatre. I could tell you what it was, but I may get a knock on the door.

Anyway, I was recruited into a team of specialists headed by one of the top engineers – our objective was to modify, test and supply an upgraded weapon before deployment.

The Engineers consulted each other about achieving the objective, how modifications to the breach, barrel, rifling, cartridge and sights could achieve the result. Various changes were made at huge expense, we worked into the night to make the modifications and made components from scratch to accommodate the design changes – but after a few weeks we were getting nowhere.

In the Special Weapons Department – or shed – there was an old guy who had the job of simply cleaning up. Bill would sweep the floor, empty the bins and generally keep the place tidy. During the course of the project he came to know what we were up to, and on one morning he said to the Lead Engineer that he could solve the problem we were facing and that he knew how to modify the weapon.

The Lead Engineer simply smiled and suggested that Bill should get back to doing what he did best while leaving the experts to sort out the technical stuff...

As time passed, deployment was getting closer and we didn't have a weapon suitable for use – we were running out of time. The Lead Engineer was becoming desperate – of all the people to let down, you really don't want to let down the Parachute Regiment. They take it personally…

As the deadline was approaching, one of the team finally asked Bill for advice. Turns out Bill had been a "Desert Rat" who had fought through North Africa in WW2. He knew about combat and he knew about improvising weapons suitable for open hostile terrain.

Bill explained how with the adjustment of a couple of screws, moving a bracket and with a bit of "field engineering" the weapon could be modified. The Lead Engineer finally took Bills advice and the modification worked. The weapons were upgraded and deployed in time.

The moral of this story is that if you really want to achieve more – simply know more. Knowledge is the key, continuous learning and personal development coupled with openness to new ideas will dramatically improve your levels of output and efficiency.

How knowledge helps you achieve more.

The classic learning curve model shows not only the structure of learning, but the benefits too. This one was demonstrated to me back in the days of being an apprentice, on the virtues of continued learning and opportunities; it still holds true today.

The Learning Curve...

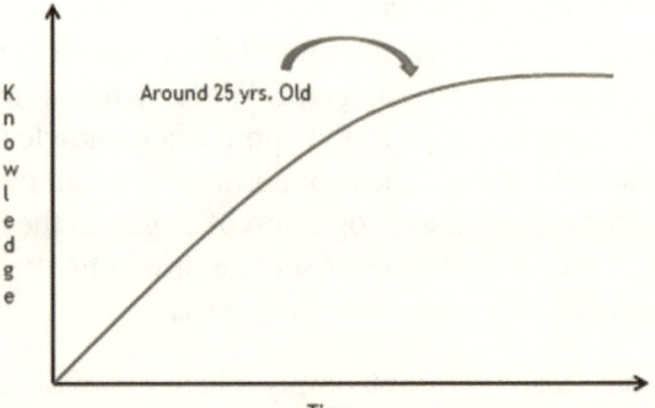

On the diagram, you can see a learning curve, from when we are born to the age of, say, twenty-five. We learn how to walk, talk, read, write, and spend our formative years becoming 'educated'. At some point, the pace of learning slows down. As we leave school or university, we don't stop learning. It is just the pace of it that slows down.

Opportunities...

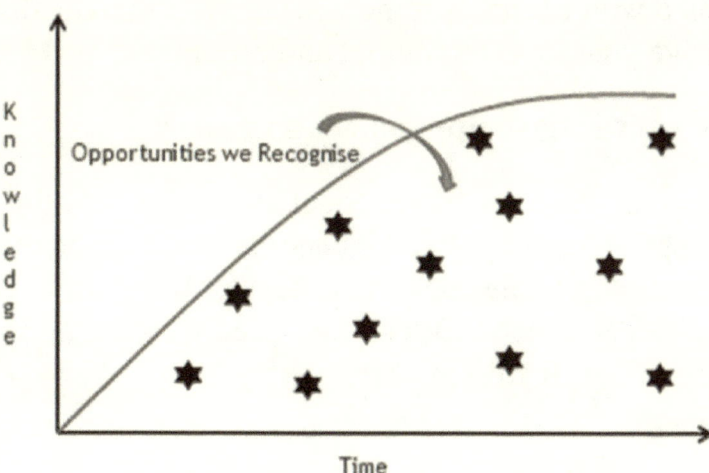

The area contained under the curve is our knowledge zone. The large black stars you can see within our knowledge zone represent opportunities that we can recognise and take advantage of. We have the ability to see them because we have the appropriate knowledge to capitalise upon them. These opportunities could be the offer of a new job, the recognition of a 'gap in the market' for a new product or service, investments, relationships, or even which car to buy.

They could also represent simply a better way of doing things; achieving more in less time with fewer resources for example.

The opportunity that was available to the Lead Engineer for example was always there – he just chose to ignore it and not allow it into his frame of reference. He didn't accept the knowledge as an opportunity and therefore couldn't see it.

Opportunities...

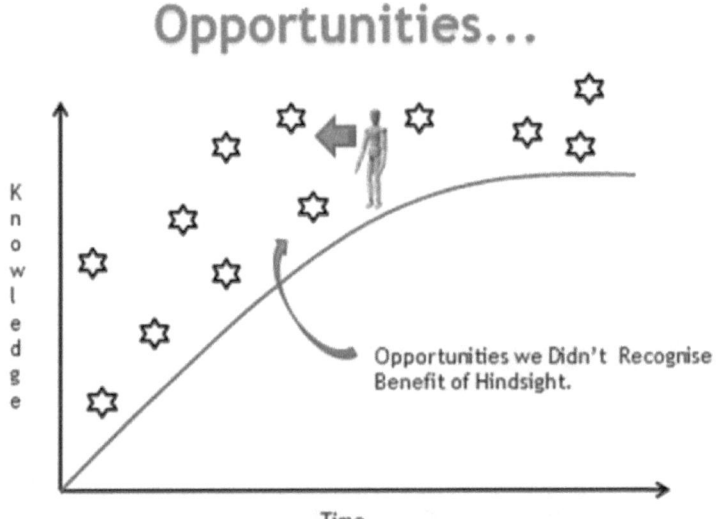

The black outlined stars on the left of the chart represent those opportunities that have passed us by because they were outside of our knowledge zone. If, as the figure demonstrates, we look back at our lives, with the benefit of both the increased knowledge we have acquired over time, and 20:20 hindsight, we can look back and see opportunities now that we simply couldn't recognise before. With hindsight, what would you change in your life if you could?

Personally, I believe that I am the sum of all my experiences. I am happy with where I am now, and therefore, I wouldn't change anything. I may change the purchase decision regarding that Fiat 131 Mirafiori in 1983 though.

Opportunities...

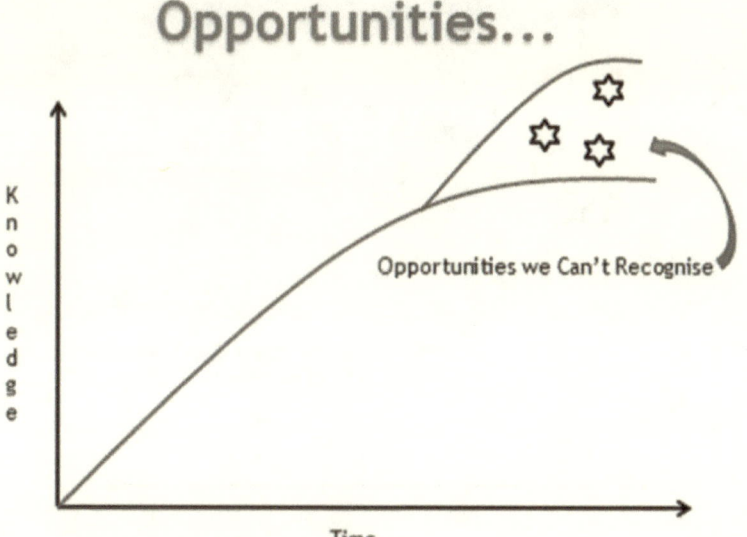

The stars on the top right of the chart represent opportunities that ordinarily are outside of our knowledge zone. We simply can't see them with what we know. The only way to capitalise on these is to accelerate our learning, expand our zone, and effectively bring them within our grasp. The small curve placed on top of the large curve represents additional knowledge which could be the result of a chance meeting, a video, or an academic course of study, a book, having a mentor, or simply a 'eureka' moment based on a change of attitude or mind-set.

So in order to achieve more, knowledge is the key – simply put – we don't know what we don't know. The fact that you are reading this, or any other book, is a great start – if you learn just one new idea and apply it, you have already expanded your knowledge zone and will see better quality opportunities...

Top Tips from this Chapter...

- **Knowledge** – allows you to recognise better opportunities.
- **Hindsight** – what would you change if you could...?
- **Ideas** – come from various sources – stay open.
- **Knowledge Zone** – what is your strategy for expanding yours...?

Notes and Action Points

The Law of Peak Condition.

I used to work in Southampton and one of my colleagues would respond to the question "how are you...?" with the answer

"I'm in the very peak of physical condition..."

Struck me at the time as being a little odd – he was an accountant, however, and was allowed and indeed expected to be somewhat strange.

He was of course correct, or at least making the correct assumption. If we want to achieve more with less then we have to look after ourselves and get in to Peak Condition; physically and mentally.

Years ago I used to ride bikes – in fact I would ride around 200 miles per week in all weathers. I was never skinny but I was reasonably fit, I would race the bus into town and win, sprint at every road sign with a distance marker, and have even cycled up Porlock Hill – the Toll Road, not the silly steep one...

Since then I have used the excuse of time, lifestyle and business commitments to relax my exercise regime, but not my carbohydrate in take regime. In short I have gained weight and become less fit – I am not at the peak of physical condition.

Of all the things that I have achieved, staying in shape has been the one I have struggled with...

What struck me was a thought one Sunday morning…

I used to train on Saturdays. Riding for 80 to 100 miles was regular – and I remember not really aching afterwards either. The thought I had was this – if I woke up one Sunday morning after having been out on one of these rides – and I was the size I am now, what would I do..?

Call a doctor, go to the A&E – overnight I would have swollen up by around 40lbs and I would want to know what had happened and how it could be reversed…

Get the fat suit off me – something would clearly have been wrong.

But what happens in reality, if we are not aware; situations creep up on us. As a species we are very tolerant and don't react to marginal imperfections – we tend to wait until catastrophe before we change.

The same happens with our approach to work; we allow bad habits and practices to enter into our daily activities. It shows up in the number of hours we work, the time we spend with family and friends, our productivity and efficiency.

The question is – what are you tolerating in terms of Health and Wellbeing – is the sacrifice of time, and balance worth the return you get in terms of income and recognition.

I was told that we can't create more time – my view is that we can. By being in Peak Condition, not only are we more effective in our roles, but we may have the opportunity of living longer to enjoy the fruits of our labour too.

What does this matter...?

I spend a lot of time travelling and delivering presentations and workshops from the stage – at last count I had been on stage in 22 countries. It is physically demanding, and in order to not just perform well, but maintain the pace, I need to get back in shape.

This applies to all of us – being healthier and fitter contributes to our levels of energy, concentration and application to our tasks and activities.

This book is not intended to be a health and wellbeing manual – I am not qualified to give advice and guidance in these areas. The simple questions for us all however include these;

Am I in the best condition, mentally and physically, that I could be...?

Do I drink too much...?

Do I smoke...?

Am I getting enough exercise...?

Is my food actually good for me...?

I have just taken on a Health Coach to help, guide and hold me accountable to a better, healthier lifestyle – it just may be that you could do the same; but only if you are serious about what you want to achieve of course...

Why is this important…?

Not that this should really need explaining, but looking after yourself is a good thing on so many levels. When you are in good physical shape, you will have more energy, be more productive and efficient and be able to achieve higher levels of output.

One of the most important aspects of being in Peak Condition is that you will not be away from work for illness as much as you might otherwise have been. I am convinced that being a Business Owner is the healthiest role anyone can have.

Taking days off for "coughs, colds, sore throats, headaches, bad back, bad leg or stress" is not an option for us – strange how owning your own business seems to cure 97.4% of all common ailments. Simply put, I love what I do too much to be sick.

Top Tips from this Chapter…

- **Health** – to operate at full potential you need to be healthy.
- **Excuses don't count** – take responsibility for you situation.
- **Creep** – over time health may deteriorate.
- **Tolerance** – what are you tolerating that you should not..?

Notes and Action Points

The Law of Planning

As we saw earlier, whilst a Vision is key, just as important is a plan to make it happen. One of the best ways of getting more done is not to do more but to STOP doing things – only doing the activities that actually take you towards your objective for example and avoiding anything else.

How do we plan for achievement and maximum effectiveness and efficiency..?

Whether the objectives are personal or professional, the same rules apply.

Your very own **Planning System** – hierarchy of actions…

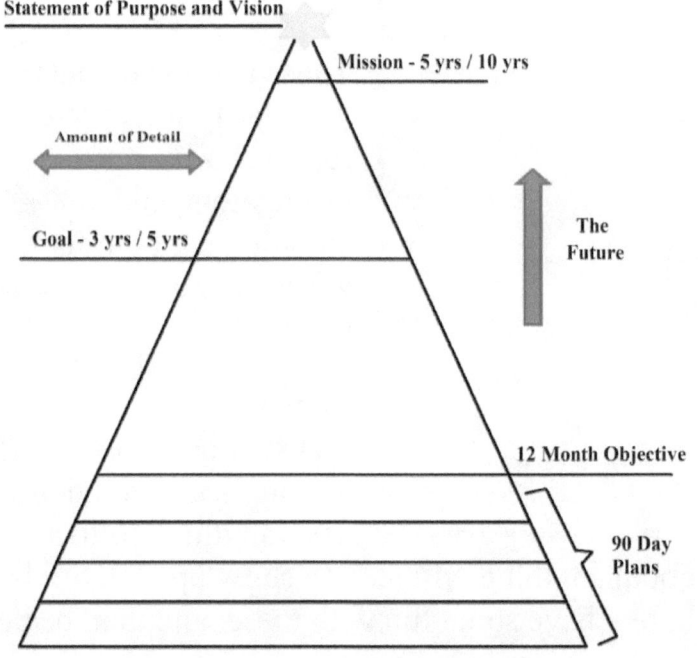

Your Statement of Purpose.

This is for you to define what your true purpose is as an individual; why are you doing what you do…?

If you run your own business, division or department, you could also produce your own Vision Statement – that defines what you will achieve professionally as a consequence of your own Purpose…

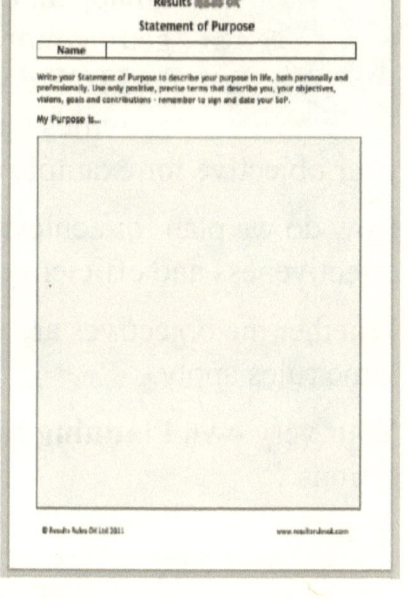

These two documents give you clarity for yourself and for your business – they will be engaging and empowering both for yourself and those around you.

Remember, if what you focus on becomes manifest to you then if you don't have anything to focus on – just about anything will tend to show up – clarity is the key here – have some fun with these, and then be bold and publish them to the world.

The Mission Statement

How will you achieve the Vision and your Purpose?

It may be for example that your Vision is similar to mine or other peoples – however, you have to choose the vehicle that you will use to take you there. I chose Business Coaching, writing and Training / Speaking for example. My Vision is to be the most effective Coach in the World and "enable everyone to enjoy learning,

achieving doing and being more..."

My Mission is to produce materials, concepts and global events that are transformational, such that people rave about the results they achieve as a consequence and we don't have to sell what we do – we have to ration it.

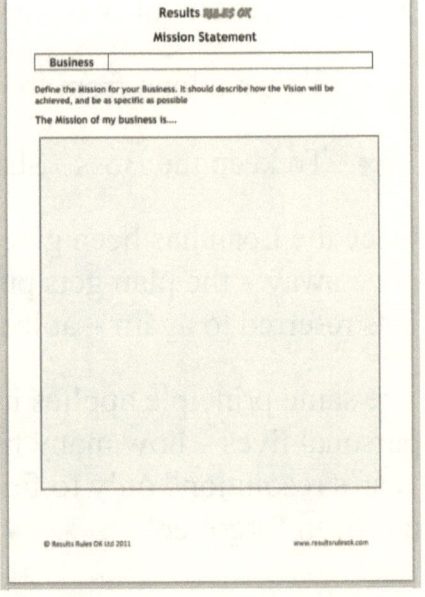

Once the Vision and Mission are clear, the Mid Term Goals and 12 Month Budgets, 90 Plans and activities are straight forwards as we know exactly what we are aiming for.

The next time you go to a company or any organisation that has the Mission Statement pinned to the wall behind the receptionist – ask people what the Mission of their organisation is.

Do they actually know what they are working towards and how they intend to achieve it…?

Is the Mission Statement simply a piece of paper that has been produced to satisfy the requirements of an ISO 9000 inspection, to comply with Investors in People or some other accreditation – or is it genuinely a guiding principle for the organisation..?

The Three Year Plan – a Single Page Business Plan

Business Plans that run into booklets are usually only produced for one of two reasons;

- To get a loan from the Bank.

- To keep the Boss / Shareholder happy.

Once the Loan has been given or the Shareholders have gone away – the plan gets put on the shelf and never gets referred to again – at least until the next meeting.

The same principle applies in business as it does to our personal lives – how many times have you made a "new year's resolution" only to find that by mid-February it has been forgotten.

To ease this situation, I'd like to recommend that every Plan should be no more than One Page long – it means it is easy to produce, can be displayed for all to see and is easy to memorise...

The principle for the Single Page Business Plan is that each year you have to define just three key objectives – highlights of achievement which represent the symptoms of everything else that you have to do.

Sales, Profit and Cash are the three drivers, and defining what they are for every quarter for the next three years is a simple way of bringing clarity to the Objectives.

To use the template as a personal or departmental tool – simply replace the headings with three other equally important headings. Could be a health and wellbeing objective for example, or a divisional or departmental performance objective – the key is that it is simple and clear…

The 12 Month Objective.

As the plans get more short term they need to get more specific and detailed.

To support your defined 12 Month Objectives you will need;

- One Page Business Plan.

- Budget / Forecast.

- Cash Flow Forecast.

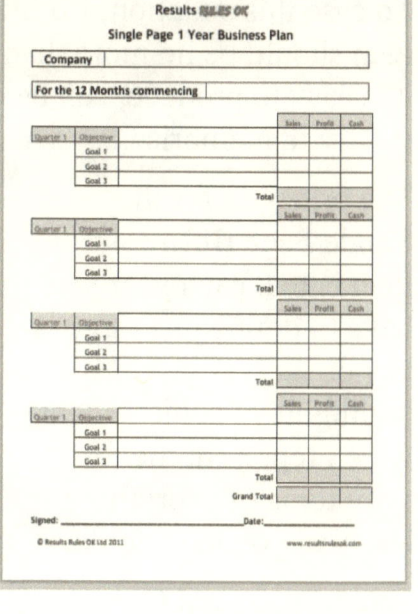

These documents are more specific and detailed – giving you a series of short term objectives that will help you keep focus and stay "on purpose" – it is the focus and purpose that defines how you invest your time.

Remember – you can't manage time – only how you allocate it…

The Budget / Forecast should be in the same format as your Management Accounts – so you can compare the results with the predictions and make the necessary adjustments as the year progresses. If anything you are doing does not contribute towards the achievement of the Budget / Forecast – then don't do it. A simple mechanism to retain focus and prevent wasted energy, time and money.

The Cash Flow Forecast will be based on the assumptions you make in the Forecast and again – should be monitored regularly to make sure you are hitting the numbers.

The Budget/Forecast

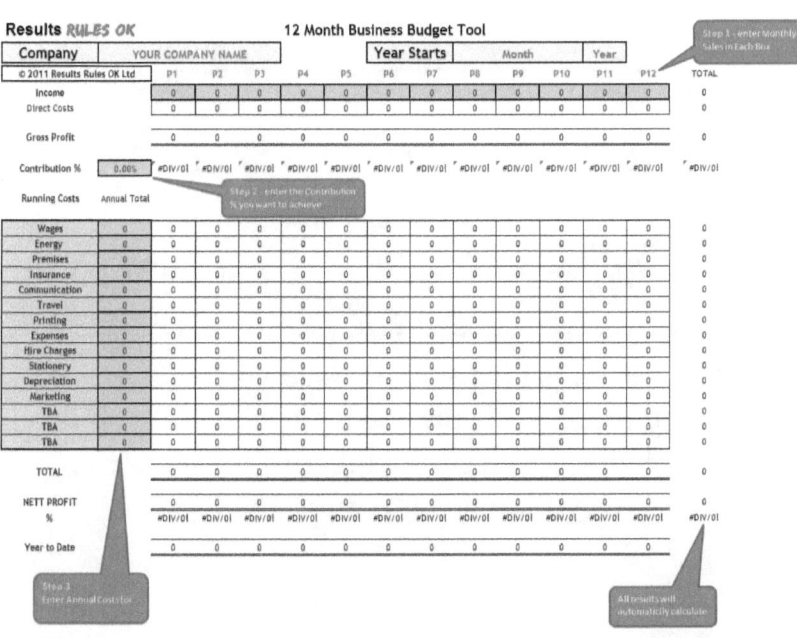

The Cash Flow Forecast

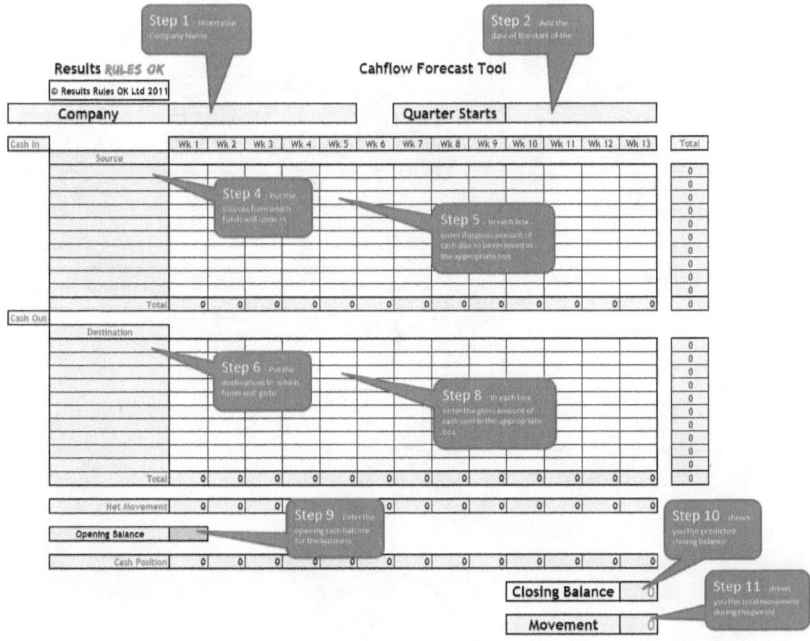

The 90 Day Plan

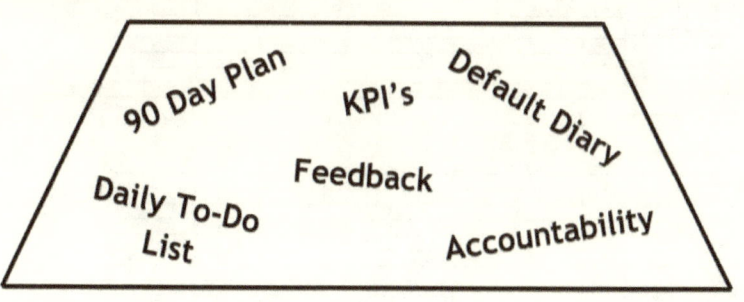

90 Day Plan | KPI's | Default Diary
Daily To-Do List | Feedback | Accountability

The 90 Day Plan is how you manage your business on an on-going basis – it is the focus for you and your team – probably helpful if every member of the team has their own 90 Day Plan in support of yours.

**Results *RULES OK*
90 Day Planning System**

Our Company

90 Days	From	To

Our Mission

_____
_____

HAVE **Targets for the next 90 Days;**

Money - _____

Other...
1 _____
2 _____
3 _____
4 _____

Reward to myself for achieving our Targets;

1 _____
2 _____
3 _____

Signed-   Date -
Name -

This Qtr	Goal 1	
	Goal 2	
	Goal 3	
DO²		Objective for the Quarter
1st 30	Goal 1	
	Goal 2	
	Goal 3	
DO²		Objective for the First Month
2nd 30	Goal 1	
	Goal 2	
	Goal 3	
DO²		Objective for the Second Month
3rd 30	Goal 1	
	Goal 2	
	Goal 3	
DO²		Objective for theThird Month

These are my BE Targets - Knowledge, Personal Development...
2
1 _____
2 _____
3 _____

© Results Rules OK

www.resultsrulesok.com

To manage the business efficiently and make the best use of time available, use a standard 90 Day Planning Template and support it with a Default Diary, Daily To-Do lists and Key Performance Indicators.

The Default Diary is where you plan all your activities – the regular ones that "must happen" on a regular basis if you are to achieve your 90 Day Plan. The same goes for you and the team – everyone needs to have a routine of activities that contributes to the achievement of the objective.

DAVID HOLLAND - DEFAULT DIARY Sample

	Monday	Tuesday	Wednesday	Thursday	Friday
0630					
0700					BNI
0730		Networking	Networking		BNI
0800		Networking	Networking		BNI
0830		Networking	Networking	COACHING	BNI
0900	E MAIL	Networking	Networking	COACHING	STRAT ALL
0930	CLIENT WORK	WALK IN'S	COACHING	COACHING	STRAT ALL
1000	CLIENT WORK	Sales Mtg	COACHING	COACHING	STRAT ALL
1030	CLIENT WORK	No 1			STRAT ALL
1100	COACHES		COACHING	COACHING	HOST BEN
1130	COACH	Sales Mtg	COACHING	COACHING	HOST BEN
1200	FEEDBACK	No 2			HOST BEN
1230	PHONE CALLS		COACHING	COACHING	BREAK
1300	BREAK	BREAK	COACHING	COACHING	ACCOUNTS
1330	PLANNING	Sales Mtg			ACCOUNTS
1400	PLANNING	No 3	BREAK	BREAK	TEAM MTG
1430	CLIENT WORK		COACHING	COACHING	TEAM MTG
1500	CLIENT WORK	Sales Mtg	COACHING	COACHING	
1530		No 4			
1600	WALK IN'S	WALK IN'S	COACHING	COACHING	
1630	WALK IN'S		COACHING	COACHING	
1700		SEMINAR			
1730	BUDDY COACH	SEMINAR	GP COACHING		
1800	CALL	SEMINAR	GP COACHING		
1830		SEMINAR	GP COACHING		
1900		SEMINAR	GP COACHING		
1930		SEMINAR	GP COACHING		
2000		SEMINAR	GP COACHING		
2030		SEMINAR	GP COACHING		
2100		SEMINAR	GP COACHING		
2130		SEMINAR	GP COACHING		

KEY

TRAVELLING
NETWORKING
CLIENT COACHING
COACHES COACH
COACHES COACH FEEDBACK
OFFICE MARKETING
SEMINAR - ONCE PER MONTH
GROUP COACHING
MEETINGS
DIAGNOSTIC MEETINGS
BREAKS

You may not plan all your time in your Default Diary – you will need clear time for ad hoc meetings and activities that crop up from time to time – but providing that you keep the basics under control – and have a set of Key Performance Indicators that can be used to measure and monitor the quality of performance achieved, you will keep on track.

And finally – have a Daily To-Do list…

At the end of each day, simply write down what you need to pick up on in the morning – this will help with relaxation, aid memory and improve efficiency. Remember to get the tough tasks out of the way first each morning – and keep to your plan.

All the tools and Templates – along with others are available **FREE** on our website, just go to www.resultsrulesok.com/sign-up.php

Top Tips from this Chapter...

- **Long Term** – have a Vision for the future, 5 or 10 years out.
- **Mid Term** – what does the next Three Years look like...?.
- **12months** – Budget and Forecast – be specific.
- **Detailed** – have your 90 Day Plan and Default Diary ready.

Notes and Action Points

The Law of Urgent, Important and Facebook

I once did some work with an Accountant whose biggest challenge was time. In a meeting one day I noticed that he was attempting to use his laptop while having a discussion with a colleague – I wondered what he was doing..

I challenged him after the meeting and discovered that he had been playing Solitaire during the meeting. I found out that he had spent around 20 hours a week playing Solitaire – his challenge wasn't time, it was application.

There are a number of different types of activities that we have to undertake, there is the routine, the exciting, the boring, the necessary and the disruptive.

When assessing how your day is going or how you are investing your time, it is a good idea to consider the quality of your activity, and what to aim for…

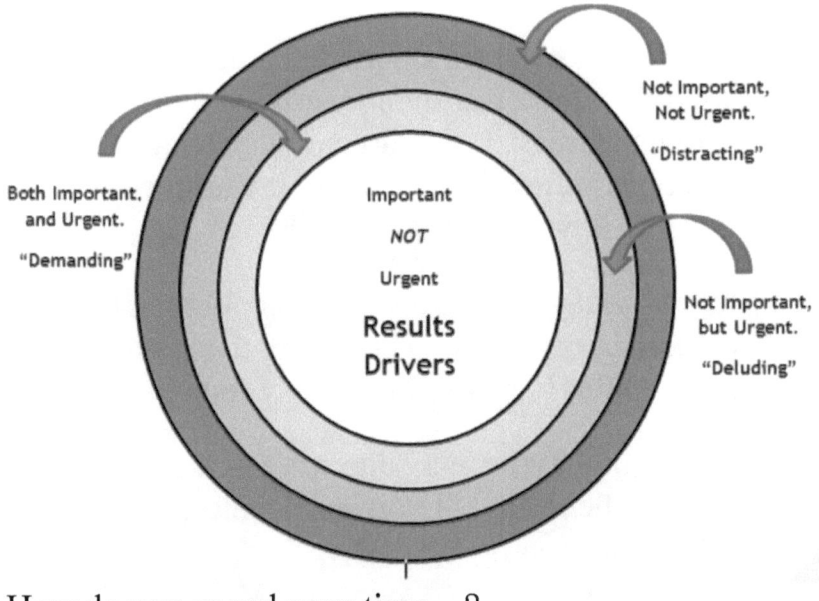

How do you spend your time…?

Not Important and Not Urgent – Distracting.

Facebook, LinkedIn, Solitaire, and other non-contributory Social Media activities are distracting you from your Objective. It may be that as part of your marketing of course you need to be on the Social Media sites – and that is fine…

What we are looking for are activities that distract – chatting, gossiping, doing private work in company time etc. Avoid these activities.

Target involvement – 0%

Not Important but Urgent – Deluding.

When we ran our own Transport Business and we had just started out, if a driver didn't show for a shift, I would drive the truck. It was urgent that the deliveries and collections were made, however it was not important that it was me that drove the vehicle.

I was "busy" and was tired and stressed – but in reality, I was deluding myself. I was not doing the highest value work that I could; I had become a busy fool.

Focus on the highest added value work you can – this is what delivers the results. If you are in Sales, then spend time selling not opening the post…

Target Involvement – 5%

Important & Urgent – Demanding.

You will have times where clients demand your attention, where a crisis occurs and you have to attend to it – these are not planned but they are predictable. In your schedule you will have to allocate time and energy to these activities.

Remember, if it was easy, everyone would do it and if everything went to plan, we wouldn't need Managers and Entrepreneurs...

Target Involvement – 25%

Important not Urgent – the Results Drivers

Writing this book was not urgent – until I committed to the team at BNY Mellon of course – but it is important. Writing books supports our Vision and Mission, it helps define what we do and attract people to us – it is really important to my business and my personal objectives that I write books, this one included.

Recognising what is important and planning for it is the single best way of investing time to the best advantage – these are the activities that move us forwards, they are the strategic rather than the tactical.

Target Involvement – 70%

Top Tips from this Chapter...

- **Don't Fool Yourself** – Urgent may not be Important.
- **Stop It** – social Media may be killing you.
- **Results Drivers** – stay here for at least 70%
- **It's OK** – to react to stuff as it happens too.

<u>Notes and Action Points</u>

The Law of Discipline

"There are two types of pain you will go through in life, the pain of discipline and the pain of regret. Discipline weighs ounces while regret weighs tonnes."

Jim Rohn

W Edwards Deming was an American Statistician, Professor, Author and Lecturer. He was born on October 14th 1900, and died on December 29th 1993. In 1947, with the Allied Powers still occupying Japan he was invited by the United States Department of the Army to go there to help out with the planning of the forthcoming census due to take place in 1951.

While he was there he was invited by the Japanese Union of Scientists and Engineers to teach their members about the principles of Statistical Process Control, SPC, From June to December 1950, he trained hundreds of engineers and managers about the concepts of SPC and also his philosophy that improving quality of manufactured goods would actually reduce expenses, increase productivity and improve market share.

Arguably it was W Edwards Deming teachings that had a profound effect on the ability of the Japanese to rebuild their economy, in Japan now the prestigious Deming Prize continues to be awarded for excellence in quality control and management. In 1960 Dr Deming was awarded the Order of the Sacred Treasure, Second

Class, in recognition of his contribution to the transformation of Japanese Industry.

In his book, Out of the Crisis, he defines 14 key principles for management, and is largely credited with the introduction of the concept of Total Quality Management.

One of the key aspects of the transformation of Japanese products was not improved design or marketing, they simply made products that were marginally better. When Ford began using Japanese manufactured gearboxes, in addition to ones made in the USA, in their cars, they noticed that customers started specifying the Japanese built units over the ones manufactured in the USA; they were even prepared to wait until a Japanese built unit was available if that was what it took.

Ford engineers could not understand what was going on, the gearboxes built in Japan were built to the same engineering drawings that were being used in the USA, so why the perceived difference. The difference it turns out was only marginal, however, it was this marginal change that delivered huge improvements to the actual quality of the gearbox. The cars with Japanese gearboxes were quieter, smoother, there was less vibration. They didn't leak oil and they lasted longer.

In 1982, after he had returned to the USA he published his book titled Out of the Crisis and he defined his 14 Key Principles for transforming business effectiveness;

- ✓ Create constancy of purpose toward improvement of product and service.

- ✓ Adopt the new philosophy.

- ✓ Cease dependence on mass inspection.

- ✓ End the practice of awarding business on the basis of a price tag alone.

- ✓ Improve constantly and forever the system of production and service.

- ✓ Institute training and retraining.

- ✓ Institute leadership.

- ✓ Drive out fear.

- ✓ Break down barriers between staff areas.

- ✓ Eliminate slogans, exhortations, and targets for the work force.

- ✓ Eliminate Numerical Quotas.

- ✓ Remove barriers to pride of workmanship.

- ✓ Institute a vigorous program of education and retraining.

- ✓ Take action to accomplish the transformation.

Although he didn't use the term, he is credited with being the "father of Total Quality Management" and introducing the philosophy of Kaizen – continuous improvement - to industry.

So what does this have to do with you being able to achieve more and still have the weekend off…?

It means that we need to focus on the causes of better productivity and efficiency, not the symptoms – a disciplined approach to the 10 Laws on a consistent basis is the best way to make a difference.

Deming's work was focussed on the inputs to a system not the outputs. He knew that if the inputs were managed and improved, the outputs would essentially look after themselves.

This is why, in my view, most traditional Time Management techniques simply don't work. They focus on managing the outcomes, not the inputs; the symptoms not the causes.

The key is consistency and discipline – to apply the strategies that will help you achieve more.

What McDonalds know about Time Management?

It's not just McDonalds; it's the whole of the Franchise industry…

A Franchise is simply a proven system of delivering a product or service that is rented to people so that, providing they follow the "system" they will achieve predictable results in terms of sales and profit – that is why people pay money for a Franchise; because the risks are less than starting from scratch.

The challenge I have seen with Franchises fall into two main categories;

- The System is not "proven" and needs to be adapted to suit the individual Franchisee. Not really a Franchise then.

- The Franchisee decides that they know better and "personalises" the system to suit their own style.

Both of these situations – or better still a combination of the two – will destroy a Franchise. The challenge we have in the realm of achieving more in the time we have is that the "system" is not defined. The 10 Laws need to be applied in a way that supports you – this is not a Franchise.

So whilst a disciplined, consistent approach to the application of the strategies that will help you is critical – it is the design of your own system that will dictate your success.

The best place to start is by doing an "audit" – you may find that you have some of the 10 Laws covered and you just need to keep doing what you are already doing; you may also find that there are a few that need attention.

Building your "system" is the key to your success – what strategies and tactics work for me or others may not work for you – you have to design your own, and then you have to use them in a consistent and disciplined manner.

Build your own Franchise for achieving more and still having weekends off; develop a set of strategies that support you. Build your Vision, develop a plan, apply the Laws and enjoy the results. Stay in the "Green Zone" and become for efficient and productive as a result – but above all enjoy the ride and take control.

The templates included at the end of this book can be used to start your audit – simply work through each of the 10 Laws and rank your performance on a scale of 1 to 10 – then write out your Action Plan that will enable you to start to take control.

Remember – the act of writing your Goals and Actions down is the best way to start. When you write something down you will make a psychological contract with yourself, and will be much more likely to keep to it. Ideas are fine but documents are better…

Top Tips from this Chapter...

- **Deming** – was a genius.
- **System** – build one and stick to it.
- **McDonalds** – get 17 year Olds to run a Global Corporation.
- **Audit** – use the template to see how you are doing.

Notes and Action Points

The Law of NO

Just say NO…

The final Law, whilst being perhaps the shortest one to describe – is the most influential.

If anything it will determine your ability to become more efficient and productive – and have the weekend off, it is your ability to stop saying Yes to everything and politely decline the opportunity to work like a dog on projects that are either delegated to you, or dropped on you by the incompetence of those around you.

It is interesting looking back to when we started this business, in fact any of the businesses that we have started over the years, from Recruitment and Transport to Training and Coaching. The number of people who come up with "opportunities" to partner, invest joint venture or become an "alliance partner" with is truly astounding.

If we had said YES to all of them, we would have been out of business within 6 months. We have learned to be selective about who we work with, what partners we align with and which clients we deliver programs and events for.

In the early stages of any business, it is very tempting to simply say yes to just about any offer that comes in – regardless of quality. We had an offer for a guaranteed 10 days' Training every month at a great day rate for example.

Financially this would have been great – but the work didn't support our Vision, and we declined.

We were also approached by a company who wanted me to build an International Franchise with them – but it meant losing control and working with people with different values and objectives. We are not in this business for just the money; we are in this business to enable everyone to enjoy learning, achieving doing and being more.

Say NO to those activities that disrupt the quality and balance of your professional and personal life – take responsibility for your life and if you need to change the environment you are in so that you can get what you want – then stop moaning about the time you don't have and make a decision to change your environment to one in which you can.

Results RULES OK
The 10 Laws of Achieving More - Audit and Action Plan

	Applicable Law	Action
1	Management	
2	Vision	
3	Efficiency & Productivity	
4	Circadian Rhythms	
5	Knowledge	
6	Peak Condition	
7	Planning	
8	Urgent, Important & Facebook	
9	Discipline	
10	No	

Signed: _____ Date:_____

Top Tips from this Chapter...

- **Just Say No** – stop being a doormat.
- **Stop It** – stopping is as important as starting.
- **Confidence** – don't be bullied in to a Yes.
- **System** – define your system, you plan and stick to it.

Notes and Action Points

About Results Rules OK

Results Rules OK was created with a simple and clear 2020 vision;

To enable everyone to enjoy learning, achieving, doing and being more...

This is achieved through the delivery of World Class Business Coaching, Training, and Development Programs designed for business owners and entrepreneurs just like you…

We recognise that all businesses are different, as are the people that build, own and run them so we have a range of products and programs that will help, inspire and support you – whatever stage of development your business is at…

You can register for our newsletter, check out David's latest blog and even download documents and templates from our website at www.resultsrulesok.com

If you'd like to come along to an event – either to join one of our Webinars or participate in a Workshop or Seminar – visit our website www.resultsrulesok.com to find our full schedule of events.

David is offers a limited number of FREE **Business Strategy Sessions** for qualifying businesses, to arrange a meeting or discussion with David, simply got to www.resultsrulesok.com, scroll down and press the **"Book Free Session with David"** button...

Our USP is our people, our delivery, the results our Clients achieve and our philosophy of Fun in Life and in Business. We are a growing profitable business, and we believe in making contributions to charity and causes that are aligned with our values.

David's unique experience, background and passion for adding value to the business and personal lives of others have enabled him to become not only a top Business Coach, but an accomplished Speaker and Author. Having worked in 21 countries so far, his presentations and key note presentations are compelling, informative and fun and his books reflect his knowledge and personality…

David's first two books are available now…

If you have got this far then maybe we should talk…!

Contact Us;

Web – www.resultsrulesok.com

Email – info@resultsrulesok.com

Other Books by David Holland now available

Business Results Rules OK Volume I

Business Results Rules OK Volume II

Life Results Rules OK Volume I

Only Read at 4am

Would you like Fries with That?

Is Business Coaching Hornswoggle

Learning How to Fly

Unlucky for Some

The Case of the Ego in the Corner

The YOU Tree

Lights, Camera, Action

Contrary to Popular Belief

Every Day in Every Way, I'm Getting Better & Better

Success Matters

Success Rules OK

Scared of the Dark?

Leads United

Selling & Closing

The Franchise Connection

The Professional Tarot

Goals, Objectives and Precession

How to Surf the Tsunami…

Strength in Numbers….

Dutch Courage...

Negotiating Success

The 9 Rules

Drumming and the Art of Business Maintenance

The 5 P's Professionals need to know

Growing Pains

Fractional Thinking

Customers for Life

Presenting Excellence

Goals Suck

Excellence is a Real Pitch

So Good they Rationed it

Getting Picked

Changing Rooms

Smoke, Mirrors and Overnight Success

The End is Nigh

Symbiotic Results

Back to Front Leadership

Seeing is Not Believing

The Silence of the Pigs

Questions from your Favourite Teenager

The 4 Keys to Build *Your* Remarkable Business

The How 2 Series

Results *RULES OK*

The *you* Tree

Business Coaching
FOR **Professionals**
BY **Professionals**

Looking for someone inspirational, competent but also kind & honest? He's THE guy. A true leader that's always there to make you better.'

"David Holland MBA is FUN, he is extremely engaging and shares his wisdom generously with an intent to always be of service to others."

'David is always able to add just the right bit of humour to his professional endeavours'

'David is a superb coach with extensive business experience and knowledge - oh, and one of the funniest people I have ever met! '

www.resultsrulesok.com

www.ingramcontent.com/pod-product-compliance
Lightning Source LLC
Chambersburg PA
CBHW022126170526
45157CB00004B/1778